The Gateless Gate

and

Polishing the Moon Sword

The Gateless Gate
and
Polishing the Moon Sword

Dane Cervine

Saddle Road Press

The Gateless Gate and Polishing the Moon Sword
© 2018 Dane Cervine

All rights reserved. No part of this book may be reproduced or transmitted in any form or by any means without written permission of the author.

Saddle Road Press
Hilo, Hawai'i
saddleroadpress.com

Cover image and book design by Don Mitchell

ISBN 978-0-9969074-8-4

"Polishing the Moon Sword" won 2nd Prize in the 2013 Morton Marcus Poetry Contest, and was published in *phren-Z*.

"A Good Death," "Old Nurse," "Abandoned Old Woman," "Getting Free of the Gods," and "Fisticuffs," appeared in *Miramar*.

"Poem of the Body," "Moon of the Red Cliffs," "Michizane Composes a Poem by Moonlight," "Joshu's Dog," and "A Rose by Any Another Name" appeared in the *Monterey Poetry Review*.

"Waking to the Dark" appeared in CATAMARAN *Literary Reader*.

Calligraphy facing p. 54 reads "Deeper. Deeper. Thunderous Silence. Thunderous Silence."

Contents

PREFACE ... 9

THE GATELESS GATE

KOAN 1 — JOSHU'S "MU" ... 14
   JOSHU'S DOG SPEAKS ... 15
KOAN 2 — HYAKUJO'S FOX ... 16
   THE FOX ... 17
KOAN 3 — GUTEI'S FINGER ... 18
   UNCLE GUS AND THE BOY ... 19
KOAN 4 — A BEARDLESS FOREIGNER ... 20
   FIVE O'CLOCK SHADOW ... 21
KOAN 5 — MAN UP IN A TREE ... 22
   ANOTHER HOUDINI'S LAST TRICK ... 23
KOAN 6 — BUDDHA TWIRLS A FLOWER ... 24
   FLOWER POWER ... 25
KOAN 7 — WASH YOUR BOWL ... 26
   SCAM ... 27
KOAN 8 — KEICHU'S WHEEL ... 28
   ZEN AND THE ART OF MOTORCYCLE MAINTENANCE ... 29
KOAN 9 — A BUDDHA BEFORE HISTORY ... 30
   WAITING FOR EVERYMAN ... 31
KOAN 10 — SEIZEI ALONE AND POOR ... 32
   COMEDY ROUTINE ... 33
KOAN 11 — JOSHU SEES THE HERMITS ... 34
   WHO'S YOUR DADDY? ... 35
KOAN 12 — ZUIGAN CALLS "MASTER" ... 36
   KNOCK-KNOCK JOKE ... 37
KOAN 13 — TOKUSAN CARRIES HIS BOWLS ... 38
   THE STING ... 39
KOAN 14 — NANSEN CUTS THE CAT IN TWO ... 40
   PROBLEMS WITH THE MOON ... 41

KOAN 15 — TOZAN'S SIXTY BLOWS	42
THE HORSE WHISPERER	43
KOAN 16 — BELLS AND ROBES	44
THE DRY CLEANERS	45
KOAN 17 — THE THREE CALLS OF THE EMPEROR'S TEACHER	46
BETRAYAL	47
KOAN 18 — TOZAN'S THREE POUNDS OF FLAX	48
SHIT HAPPENS	49
KOAN 19 — ORDINARY MIND IS THE WAY	50
THESE BOOTS WERE MADE FOR WALKING	51
KOAN 20 — A MAN OF GREAT STRENGTH	52
WHEN THE CARNIVAL COMES TO TOWN	53
KOAN 21 — UMMON'S SHIT-STICK	56
IN CASE YOU THINK THIS IS METAPHOR	57
KOAN 22 — KASHO AND THE FLAGPOLE	58
HALF-MAST IS NOT ENOUGH	59
KOAN 23 — THINK NEITHER GOOD NOR EVIL	60
HIDE & SEEK	61
KOAN 24 — WITHOUT WORDS, WITHOUT SILENCE	62
NON-SEQUITUR	63
KOAN 25 — TALK BY THE MONK OF THE THIRD SEAT	64
NAKED AND DREAMING	65
KOAN 26 — TWO MONKS ROLL UP THE BAMBOO BLINDS	66
TWINS	67
KOAN 27 — NEITHER MIND NOR BUDDHA	68
MONOPOLY	69
KOAN 28 — RYUTAN BLOWS OUT THE CANDLE	70
WAKING TO THE DARK	71
KOAN 29 — NEITHER THE WIND NOR THE FLAG	72
BEYOND THE EYE	73
KOAN 30 — THIS VERY MIND IS THE BUDDHA	74
SOMEWHERE OVER THE RAINBOW	75
KOAN 31 — JOSHU SEES THROUGH THE OLD WOMAN	76
CITY SLICKER	77
KOAN 32 — QUESTIONING THE BUDDHA	78
BE CAREFUL WHAT YOU ASK FOR	79
KOAN 33 — NO MIND, NO BUDDHA	80
BARGAINING	81

KOAN 34 — MIND IS NOT THE WAY	82
TREASURE MAP	83
KOAN 35 — SEIJO'S SOUL SEPARATED	84
THE ONE SEIJO	85
KOAN 36 — WHEN YOU MEET A MAN OF THE WAY	86
BEST FRIENDS	87
KOAN 37 — JOSHU'S OAK TREE	88
STRAIGHT TALK	89
KOAN 38 — AN OX PASSES THE WINDOW	90
OX-TAIL MIND	91
KOAN 39 — YOU HAVE MISSED IT	92
THE IMPERSONATOR	93
KOAN 40 — TIPPING OVER A WATER PITCHER	94
CHARADES	95
KOAN 41 — BODHIDHARMA AND PEACE OF MIND	96
ZEN BOOT CAMP	97
KOAN 42 — A WOMAN COMES OUT OF MEDITATION	98
ALL I REALLY NEED TO KNOW I LEARNED IN KINDERGARTEN	99
KOAN 43 — SHUZAN AND A STAFF	100
A ROSE BY ANY OTHER NAME	101
KOAN 44 — BASHO AND A STICK	102
SHTICK	103
KOAN 45 — WHO IS HE?	104
MISSING PERSON	105
KOAN 46 — STEP FORWARD FROM THE TOP OF A POLE	106
MUD ZEN	107
KOAN 47 — TOTOTSU'S THREE BARRIERS	108
THREE GATES	109
KOAN 48 — KEMPO'S ONE ROAD	110
ONE ROAD	111

POLISHING THE MOON SWORD

A GOOD DEATH	116
MICHIZANE COMPOSES A POEM BY MOONLIGHT	117
THE MOON OF THE MILKY WAY	118
TSUNENOBU AND THE DEMON	119
TZU YU'S LAMENT	120
CLOTH-BEATING MOON	121

Return to Moon Palace	122
Mount Miyagi Moon	123
Moon of the Red Cliffs	124
Blind Moon	125
Lonely Moon	126
New Moon Grief	127
Mad Moon	128
Poem of the Body	129
Moon of the Filial Son	130
Wolf Moon Musician	131
Fisticuffs	132
Getting Free of the Gods	133
The Moon's Four Strings	134
Exile	135
Cassia Tree Moon	136
The Broken Water Bucket	137
Eclipse Moon of Lady Iga	138
Traveling Together	139
Five Beauties	140
Famous Places	141
Thirty-Six Poets	142
The Forests of Mount Fuji	143
Moon of the Vengeful Ghosts	144
Abandoned Old Woman	145
Old Nurse	146
Koan Moon	147
Lucky Moon	148
Acknowledgments	149
About the Author	151

Preface

THE GATELESS GATE, or *Mumonkan,* is one of the great classics in the literature of Zen Buddhism. It is a collection of 48 *koans,* ancient stories and sayings of Chinese Zen masters used to embody the paradoxical spirit of Zen. The Gateless Gate was composed in 1228 by the monk Mumon Ekai. He gathered this set of essential koans that had been taught for centuries, adding to each a commentary and a poem. Often terse, enigmatic, surreal, these koans have jostled open many a Zen monk's mind to an experience of life that is beyond words. Much like a poem.

There is a long tradition of composing poems as a spontaneous, personal response to koans. They deepen contemplation and illustrate the innumerable threads of any single koan. Zen is a tradition that values no-words, yet its history is littered, some would say, with the "vice" of poems. Wang Wei and Su T'ung-po were Zen practiners and poets. Po Chu-i "inked a lot of rice paper"— over three thousand of his poems survive. In "Madly Singing in the Mountains," he calls poetry his "special failing."

Perhaps this can be our special failing too, as koans make their way in a new land, a new century. There is a very formal koan-study tradition in the Rinzai school of Zen. The Soto school also uses koans, in a more informal manner.

Zen masters are famous for rejecting the answers that students bring them, often for years on end. It is not because they have brought the "wrong answer." Sometimes their answer exists only in the intellect, unembodied. There is no "right" answer to a koan, although there is a catalogue of acceptable responses to koans that was concocted to act as a basic guide. This is reminiscent of attempts to educate students in the "correct" way to read a poem. I think of the scene in *Dead Poets Society,* where Robin Williams instructs his startled students to take their rulers, place them firmly on the spine of the book about "how to read poetry," and rip the introduction out. There is something more in a koan, as in a poem, than literal understanding.

The poems in this book vary in voice and humor, expressing some of the irascible irreverence of the koan tradition itself. Mixing contemporary with ancient images, each is a response to some kernel in the koan, an edge of something, an opening. They are often humorous, or surreal, like the koans themselves. No poem here is the right answer to anything.

Koans and poems shouldn't use slang or jargon that keeps others "outside." Demystifying some of the culture-specific references of a koan can help its innate evocativeness to arise, rather than simply being impenetrable to the lay-person's ear.

Dr. A.V. Grimstone, in his introduction to Katsuki Sekida's translation of The Gateless Gate, says:

Indeed, translated into English…(koans) are in some ways easier to understand than they are in the original, because by its very nature the English language imposes a degree of clarity that is avoidable in Chinese. (The price of such a gain in clarity is some loss of richness and depth.)

This may give us hope that we can respond to these ancient koans in our own way. It is the path of both Zen and poetry, like water, to find new shapes in new contexts.

In a letter from Nakagawa Soen to Senzaki Nyogen in 1938, as the teachings of the Gateless Gate began to make their way across the Pacific, the old master says,

> *I feel emancipated just seeing the teaching conveyed in Roman letters rather than Japanese ideograms. Zen, which is fundamentally about the emancipation of all beings, is unfortunately sealed in some square box called Zen. In this enclosure the ancient dog in the koan…"Mu" has been suffocating. In English this dog is so joyfully alive!"*

Perhaps the one prohibition when encountering a koan, or a poem, can be found in Mumon's "Zen Warnings" in the appendix to The Gateless Gate: To not be a "dead man breathing." He goes on to say, "Now tell me, what will you do?" This book of poems is a way for me to live inside of this question.

Polishing The Moon Sword, which follows this collection of 48 new koan poems, represents a different tack: prose poems based on ancient Japanese and Chinese folk tales. As with the koan poems, they focus on a single moment. But these poems also deal with the age-old questions of love, aging, death, loss, and beauty. Each prose poem is meant to embody a kind of Jungian archetypal meaning akin to a koan, where the characters are more than their tale—as our own lives may be. Woven in the simple, spare lines of the prose poem are mirrors of our own psyches—perhaps their own *gateless gate* into mystery. While these tales originated in the historical landscapes of another culture, as metaphor and archetype they nonetheless may open doors within the reader.

Note: Chinese names are generally given in their Japanese form in these koans. Every translator handles this differently. Since much of the Zen tradition received by the West has come through Japanese teachers, a number of the initial koan books have utilized this method. In addition, I have often integrated several translations of individual koans according to my own poetic ear, and have relied heavily on the following books:

Nyogen Senzaki and Paul Reps, "The Gateless Gate," in *Zen Flesh, Zen Bones,* ed. Paul Reps (Rutland, Vermont, and Tokyo: Tuttle 1957).

Zenkei Shibayama, *Zen Comments on the Mumonkan,* trans. Sumiko Kudo (New York: Harper & Row, 1974).

Katsuki Sekida, *Two Zen Classics: The Gateless Gate and The Blue Cliff Records,* (Shambala, Boston & London, 2005).

Also, this poetry collection includes only the core koans of the Gateless Gate; the additional commentary, verse, and appendix by Mumon Ekai, and translators, can be found in the Shibayama and Sekida books just noted.

>Dane Cervine
>Santa Cruz, California

The Gateless Gate

Koan 1 — Joshu's "Mu"

A monk asked Joshu, "Has a dog Buddha Nature or not?" Joshu answered, "Mu!"

Joshu's Dog Speaks

No, is all I hear, all day long
because the poor monk won't shut up.
Some Zen master too. He knows
I'm more Buddha than this ornery student
will ever be: smells too clean, never looks at me directly.
But my master keeps trying, gotta love him for that…
Mu, Mu, Mu, to every question the asshole asks.
Don't get me wrong, I love assholes—they're
my main way of finding out what's going on
in the world, around the corner, on the next
block. But isn't it obvious, I mean my master's
answer? It's just his way of barking, like
Shut the fuck up, it's not even a question, man!
There's only one nature, it's not hard to follow.
Just stick your nose to the ground, follow the scent,
spray your own to accent the fragrance
of the other's spot, keep going.
Lick your privates now and then.
It's called *The Way,* man.

Koan 2 — Hyakujo's Fox

"Who are you standing here before me?" Hyakujo said to the old man in the meditation hall that no one else could see. "I am not a human being. I used to be a head monk, living here on this mountain eons ago. One day a student asked me, *Is a man of enlightenment subject to the law of causation or not?* I answered, *No he is not*. Since then I have endured five hundred rebirths as a fox. Tell me, does a man of enlightenment fall under this yoke of causation or not?" Hyakujo answered, *He is one with causation*. At that, the old fox was enlightened, and said "Please bury my body as that of a dead monk". Later, Hyakujo led all the monks from the meditation hall to the foot of a rock on the far side of the mountain and with his staff poked at the dead body of a fox, then performed the ceremony of cremation for a monk who has passed over.

The Fox

Déjà vu, dying again. After so much
beauty beneath these White Pines,
one life after another,
haunting the chicken coops in the village,
nose-deep in blood and feather,
ten thousand scents flooding my nostrils.
More drunk with it than half the monks
snoring in the Zendo, oblivious
to the obvious: there is no escape.
Who would want to?
Five hundred precious births,
four hundred ninety-nine deaths.
Such good fortune. And now
an old man in black robes pokes my body
with his sharp stick as the mist
enshrouds the mountain. Here
I go again, though this time
my gnarled bones and sinew
are not sinking into the hillside.
For some reason, the old man
has thrown me on the fire.
I am smoke, and crackle.
I could be anything.

Koan 3 — Gutei's Finger

Gutei raised his finger whenever he was asked a question about Zen. A boy attendant began to imitate him. Gutei heard about the boy's mischief, seized him, cut off his finger. The boy cried and ran away. Gutei called and stopped him. When the boy turned his head, Gutei again raised up his own finger. In that instant, the boy was enlightened.

Before dying, Gutei gathered the monks around him, said "I attained my finger-Zen from my teacher, and in my whole life could not exhaust it." Then he passed away.

Uncle Gus and the Boy

It's the oldest trick in the book,
but one they'll remember: grasp
the left thumb with the right hand,
fold it under the knuckle
just as the knife slices a piece
of you away. The opposing
thumb, deftly lifted in place,
quickly detached then re-attached
like a magician up close, plain
for all to see. Zen masters
are like uncles, or magicians,
not to be trusted except
with the things that matter. Like
the one thing the boy must know,
that can never be exhausted.
This sleight of hand.

There is only one finger.
It is all that matters.

Koan 4 — A Beardless Foreigner

Wakuan complained when he saw a picture of bearded Bodhidharma, the tattooed Indian with big eyes who brought Zen to China from India: "Why hasn't that fellow a beard?"

Five O'Clock Shadow

The mirror never lies. He runs
his smooth palm over the late
afternoon stubble. No,
it would never be more
than his own brand of shadow,
though he longs to be
like this guru with the red fire beard
tumbling down his chest.
To feel enlightened in every muscle
of his odd body just like the Zen heroes
with their superhuman powers
and cool confidence—
this is the thing he can never master.
Still, he is getting used to being himself.
The mirror a better reflection
than the tattered scroll with the wild
man from India's bug eyes,
enigmatic tattoos. It would be fun
to be enlightened—but not like this,
with a big red flame of beard
when you really love the razor,
the hair in the sink, the way
your original face feels.

Koan 5 — Man Up in a Tree

Kyogen said: "Zen is like a man hanging in a tree by his teeth over a precipice. His hands grasp no branch, his feet rest on no limb, and under the tree another person asks him, *Why did Bodhidharma come to China from India?* If the man in the tree does not answer, he fails; and if he does answer, he falls and loses his life. Now what shall he do?"

Another Houdini's Last Trick

You're hanging by your teeth,
the spotlight glaring,
the stage tree surprisingly real,
the leather harness tethering you
to the branch invisible to the audience
gasping as you sway back and forth,
arms swimming the emptiness like a fish
as your lovely assistant stands beneath you
in her Las Vegas jeweled bodice shouting
Why, why, why....
Nobody really expects you to answer.
They barely understand the question—
but good money is riding on whether
true magic will happen.
Can you unhinge your jaw
from that last safety, twist
in the air and shout the one thing
you've been wanting to say
your entire staged life,
fall into the darkness beneath,
land where no one else can see,
angle toward the backstage door
into the alley, walk away
into your one true life?

Koan 6 — Buddha Twirls a Flower

When Buddha was on the mountain, he turned a flower in his fingers and held it before his listeners. Everyone was silent. Only Kasho broke out into a broad smile. The Buddha said, *I have the True Dharma Eye, the Marvelous Mind of Nirvana, the True Form of the Formless, and the Subtle Dharma Gate. It is beyond words, beyond teaching. This I have given to Kasho.*

Flower Power

The battered Volkswagen van with the psychedelic
flowers is still humming along, the old engine
in the back sounding more like a mantra each year.
I couldn't bear to part with it, though Haight-Ashbury
is just another San Francisco intersection now –
for the lost, the nostalgic, the newly enlightened.
There are so many Buddhas now
though most don't realize their own
secret identity. That's why this Dharma Bus
is so important, sporting an incandescent
Eye large enough to cover the rear door,
a glimmering Gate matching the sliding doors
on the passenger side. Drive slow enough
down the street and people stop to stare.
I don't need to say a word. I smile, they smile.
It's as though a little bit of Nirvana
bursts into petal in the furthest reaches
of their hearts. The red rose, luminous
on the flat hood, is worth ten thousand *sutras,*
ten world religions, one awakening.
Feel it vibrate down the pot-hole road,
rumble in your chest, flower.

Koan 7 — Wash Your Bowl

A monk told Joshu, "I have just entered the monastery. Please teach me." Joshu asked, "Have you eaten your rice porridge?" The monk replied, "I have eaten." Joshu said, "Then you had better wash your bowl." At that moment the monk was enlightened.

Scam

The Kamasutra Tantric Sexuality workshop
was my favorite, followed by the Kundalini
Jade Serpent-Up-The-Spine seminar,
though there's been scores of others along the way.
Gets expensive, but I'll do anything to get enlightened.
The ancient Chinese monks would wander rocky paths,
down treacherous gorges, through snow and storm
from one monastery to another, desperate
to find a teacher who would share the secret.
At least I get to fly first class to the next week-long
retreat—though no one knows what they're talking about,
or are scamming for more money, a higher certification.
Perhaps I'm just a failure. Too tough a nut to crack.
But this new teacher made me throw in the towel.
Didn't charge much, but all week wouldn't answer
one damn question directly, and I had big questions.
Important ones. He just kept asking if I'd washed my bowl
after dinner, made my bed, helped weed the garden,
remembered to breathe, like, all the time.
If I loved myself as though I were the last human
on the face of the Earth. Of course, I failed
that last one. Just looked in his big ole' moon eyes,
surrendered. No more scams. That's when it hit me,
you know? How much I loved the blanket on my bed,
the wildflowers in the garden, my old bowl,
this moon in our eyes.

KOAN 8 — KEICHU'S WHEEL

Keichu, the first wheel-maker of China, made two wheels of fifty spokes each. Now, suppose you removed the nave uniting the spokes. What would become of the wheel? And had Keichu done this, could he be called the master wheel-maker?

Zen and the Art of Motorcycle Maintenance

The orange paperback book still fits
in the back pocket of my jeans.
I glance at the well-thumbed pages
when remembering the art and science of no-self,
but by now it's second-nature.
This dismantling of the entire machine—
every piston, gear, bolt,
the leather seat, the chrome handlebars,
the immense road-hugging rubber tires,
the immaculate silver spokes radiating
from the center hub like lightning. All of it
laid across the cement floor of the monastery
of my mind—to be cleaned, polished, re-oiled,
put back together as the comfortable cruiser
this old speed demon body has become. Gone
the glory days, *mano a mano* drag races,
careening towards the black & white flag,
the woman with the jade eyes at the finish line.
There's nothing there behind the flag, the iris,
at the center of anything. But oh, this ride.
There's nothing like it. Wind, trees, the road
in the rearview mirror, the road ahead,
the road right under my feet like thunder.

Koan 9 — A Buddha Before History

A monk asked Seijo: "I understand that a Buddha who lived before recorded history sat in meditation for ten *kalpas* and did not attain Buddhahood. How could this be?" Seijo replied: "Your question is self-explanatory." The monk asked: "He meditated so long; why could he not attain Buddhahood?" Seijo said, "Because he did not become a Buddha."

Waiting for Everyman

I'm just sitting here waiting for Everyman.
　　　　　　　　—*Jackson Browne*

After the concert, I saved the ticket stub
as though it were a Tibetan prayer flag
or rosary to rub my thumb over. To always
remember how the entire audience
flicked our cigarette lighters and single matches
to flame, swayed in the blackness,
a dark ocean of folk-rock intoxicated *bodhisattvas*
vowing over every bridge, with each swelling chorus,
to help each other along—to carry the whole
damn world on our young shoulders
even if it took ten *kalpas,* even if we
never made it alone. But

even a few years made the journey seem
impossible. No matter how long I sat,
no matter how long I waited, becoming
a Buddha seemed to recede into some
unreachable future. A whole generation,
this entire species of *Homo sapiens*
still waiting. I looked for that ticket stub
in my memorabilia box the other day,
but it was gone. Perhaps worn thin
by longing till it disappeared. Yet I no longer
seem to care about arriving. It is enough
to assume the position—whether poised
on zapphu, the far bleachers of Jackson's
nostalgia tour, walking among the homeless,
the war zone of the television screen,
the mind. It is enough to be a failed
bodhisattva waiting for the Buddha
already here in Everyman.

Koan 10 — Seizei Alone and Poor

A monk named Seizei asked master Sozan: "Seizei is alone and poor. Will you give him support?" Sozan asked: "Seizei?" Seizei responded: "Yes, Sir?" Sozan said: "You have Zen, the best wine in China, and already have finished three cups. Still you are saying that they did not even wet your lips."

Comedy Routine

Two old rascals, like Laurel & Hardy
or Groucho & Harpo – Zen masters
sparring like corner Hip-Hop dharma
combatants throwing down
spoken words just to provoke
a bit of light in the dark auditorium
of this world. Don't believe a word
they say: *I am alone. I am poor. I need.*
Cantankerous old men are only interested
in one thing – at least these rascals are.
After three cups of this world,
are your lips wet? Does Napa Valley
fill your nostrils with purple,
the French Bordeaux and Alsace
with red grape and pink muscat?
Or Harlem's taverns, Sam's corner bar,
the priest's blood of Christ in a shot glass,
Rumi intoxicated by the love of Shams,
Sozan's plum wine, the samurai's sake?
If you're not drunk with this world
after all these years, what are you waiting for?
Hey you, the one with the wet lips,
can you say, *Thank you Master Sozan!*

Koan 11 — Joshu Sees the Hermits

Joshu went to a hermit's cottage and asked, "Is the master in? Is the master in?" The hermit raised his fist. Joshu said, "The water is too shallow to anchor here," and he went away. Coming to another hermit's cottage, he asked again, "Is the master in? Is the master in?" This hermit, too, raised his fist. Joshu said, "Free to give, free to take, free to kill, free to save," and he made a deep bow.

Who's Your Daddy?

The hermits don't mind the old man.
He's always joking, always testing,
showing up at their tiny shacks in the forest
at all hours, banging on the front door
peeking through holes in the boards,
throwing back the tacked cloth curtains
yelling, *Anybody home? Anyone here?*
They've learned not to say much,
you never knew what crazy thing
he might throw back. Calling you
shallow one moment, free the next.
The hermits grew to love the questions,
What does it mean to be home?
Where am I right now?
Awake, asleep, entangled?
Even in the dead of winter he'd stand
right in front of their cross-legged equanimity,
towering, bug-eyed, spitting,
Who's your daddy? But now
they just raise a single fist in the air.
The old man kind of likes this.
Smiles at their supple hands.
Breath filling the cold air
like dragon smoke.

KOAN 12 —ZUIGAN CALLS "MASTER"

Every day Master Zuigan used to call out to himself, "Oh, Master!" and would answer himself, "Yes?" "Are you awake?" he would ask, and would answer, "Yes, I am." "Never be deceived, any day, any time." "No, I will not!"

Knock-Knock Joke

When young, Zuigan stayed up all night
preparing to meet the Master. Still as a stone,
eyelids half open, Gyokuro tea to stay awake.
Finally, facing Master Ganto, he summoned
all his sincerity, his yearning, and asked
What is the Eternal Truth? He wanted
to go straight to the center, but Master
simply replied, *You have missed it!*
Stunned, he stuttered and mumbled
How did I miss it? He'd been sure
the venerable Master would elucidate
eternal truth; what good were Masters
otherwise? Slaving away in the monastery
kitchen, cleaning the toilets, sitting still
as a rock for days on end—didn't he
deserve eternal truth? It took years
till he began to glimpse that the calling
Master and the answering Master
were not two. He'd been knocking
from inside!

Koan 13 — Tokusan Carries His Bowls

One day, Master Tokusan came down to the dining room as usual, carrying his bowls. Monk Seppo said, "Old Master, the bell has not rung and the drum has not yet been struck. Where are you going with your bowls?" Tokusan at once turned back to his room. Seppo told this incident to Master Ganto, who remarked, "Great Master though he is, Tokusan has not yet grasped the last word of Zen." Hearing of it, Tokusan sent his attendant to call Master Ganto in, and asked, "Do you not approve of me?" Ganto whispered his reply to him. Tokusan was satisfied and silent. The next day Master Tokusan appeared on the rostrum. Sure enough, his talk was different from the usual ones. Master Ganto came in front of the monastery, laughed heartily, clapping his hands, and said, "What a great joy it is! The old Master has now grasped the last word of Zen. From now on, nobody in the world can ever make light of him."

The Sting

Nobody loves gossip more than a spiritual
seeker, and no one is a better mark. Seppo
thought he'd caught demented old Tokusan
tottering from his cell, empty bowls in hand,
when it wasn't even dinner yet. Some master.
Tokusan, eyeing his patsy like Paul Newman,
serenely turned back to his room. When Seppo
waddled his sitting duck Zen into the grand
set-up, Ganto, the spitting image of Robert
Redford, was ready. Hubris thick as incense
wafted between them, gossiping about how
the old man was losing it, no longer a sharp
stick. The scam laid, Paul Tokusan Newman
and Robert Ganto Redford whispered secrets
only true con men know. Still, they liked
the poor kid, he might turn into a true Zen man.
How to sting him awake was the question,
Seppo so full of himself. The next morning,
the two masters ambled on stage. Their mark
was sitting in perfect posture right up front.
Watched the old men throw down a spoken-word
Zen rap that shriveled his poor monk balls
and curled his smart tongue. Left no doubt
it was the old-school guys who laughed best.
At themselves, with each other, and finally,
he was laughing too.

KOAN 14 — NANSEN CUTS THE CAT IN TWO

Nansen saw the monks of the eastern and western halls fighting over a cat. He seized the cat and told the monks: "If any of you say a good word, you can save the cat." No one answered. So Nansen boldly cut the cat in two pieces. That evening Joshu returned and Nansen told him about this. Joshu removed his sandals and, placing them on his head, walked out. Nansen said: "If you had been there, you could have saved the cat."

Problems With The Moon

There are limits to metaphor.
This is what troubled Master Nansen,
his monks split in two factions
over how to run the monastery,
the right way to meditate, and what to do
about the wild cat that haunted the Zendo at night
crying to waxing and waning moon alike,
and who was leaving milk for it in the kitchen?
Monks are impenetrable. He knew
they might kill the poor cat he'd secretly
invited into their midst, fed with milk, sat
beside on the hillside under moons dark
and crescent, gibbous and full—to contemplate
desire's feral nature. Teachers and magicians
use the same bag of tricks—a little sleight
of hand, and *Voila!,* the cat or the woman
and hopefully the monk's mind is cut in two,
and they awaken! But not these black-robed
lacquer buckets. When Master Joshu returned
from his rounds, heard the story, all he could do
was roll his eyes, put his sandals on his head,
walk away. Nansen laughed:
*Well, if you'd been there, maybe you could have
saved these monks from themselves!*
That night, the two old men sat together
on the hill, the cat curled in their laps, purring.

Koan 15 — Tozan's Sixty Blows

Tozan came to study with Ummon, who asked: "Where are you from?" "From Sato," Tozan replied. "Where were you during the summer?" "Well, I was at the monastery of Hozu, south of the lake." "When did you leave there?" Ummon asked. "On August 25" was Tozan's reply. "I spare you sixty blows," Ummon said. The next day Tozan came to Ummon and said, "Yesterday you said you spared me sixty blows. I beg to ask you, where was I at fault?" "Oh, you rice bag!" shouted Ummon. "What makes you wander about, now west of the river, now south of the lake?" At this Tozan was enlightened.

The Horse Whisperer

The mind is a horse, and there is
never any fault in a horse. Oh sure,
there is wildness, much wandering,
skittishness at broken branches, shadows,
or lazing aimless on open ground.
The Master knows this, loves her horse –
all horses, really. But the nameless
wilderness is not where Master
and mammal meet. She knows
it is here, where bridle and saddle
wait, that a horse and a woman
or man may whisper each other's
secret names, together become
more than each alone. A bag
of oats to calm, a strong rope
at first, soft taps from riding crop,
horsehair fly whisk to spur—
till horse and rider are one. Alone,
neither would know the other. But
in this monastery of a barn, where
breath meets body, there is home.
And the wild, open fields.

Koan 16 — Bells and Robes

Ummon asked: "The world is such a wide world, why do you answer a bell and don ceremonial robes?"

The Dry Cleaners

The Master loved America. You could become
anyone. Do anything—well, within the confines
of the usual: race, gender, class wars. Nothing
new about history. But for a Buddhist dry cleaner
on the urban corner, this had to be one of the
innumerable bliss realms. Every day, someone
forgot something: faded blue jeans with holes,
Armani suit, red low-cut satin dress, Mickey-
Mouse silk tie, a Catholic priest's black garb
with pearly white collar. His favorite was
baseball uniforms, or the peach colored
polo shirts. Before laundering or dry cleaning
he'd sometimes try them on, knot Mickey's tie
round the priestly robes, even stick his thick neck
and arms through the satin dress, zip himself in.
Then sneak into the back, pull out his folding
metal chair, the meditation bell, sit for awhile.
It was good to be a Buddhist in America.
You could be anyone.

KOAN 17 — THE THREE CALLS OF THE EMPEROR'S TEACHER

The Emperor's teacher, Chu, called his successor, Oshin, three times—and three times Oshin responded. Chu said, "I long feared that I was betraying you, but really it was you who were betraying me."

Betrayal

Oshin knew Chu loved him, wanted
him to be his successor. He was happy
to come whenever called, wide awake
like a ragged puppy to his master.
He knew the tradition of *betrayal*,
surpassing your teacher's Zen
so as not to destroy half his merit.
Nights, he'd grind the inkstone
made of pine soot, animal glue,
mix with water to make black ink—
then dip the sumi-brush, practice
his calligraphy: *Ko,* meaning *to sin;*
fu, meaning to rebel. *Kofu,* to act
against his teacher's instructions,
to find his own way, to be worthy.

Koan 18 —Tozan's Three Pounds of Flax

A monk asked Master Tozan, "What is the Buddha?" Tozan said, "Three pounds of flax."

SHIT HAPPENS

What a mouth he has, thought the monk.
It's the same every time I ask:
What is the Buddha? I really, really
want to know. If I can't determine
the Buddha's sublime nature, touch
his luminous mind, what hope is there
for a poor monk? For anyone? At least
this time it was "three pounds of flax,"
not very original since I happened to be
carrying the bag, but better than his usual
irreverence comparing the Buddha
to shit, or fallen blossoms, or someone to kill.
Is he that cynical, or lazy? He smirks,
all the masters smirk, when I come round
with my sincere, studied, artful questions.
Like there's some big joke I just don't get!
As though enlightenment were just whatever
was happening in the moment. It's always
changing, how can I count on that!
I want a Golden Buddha! Not a bag of flax,
a pile of cow manure, or even peach blossoms.
Certainly not a god you have to kill!

KOAN 19 — ORDINARY MIND IS THE WAY

Joshu asked Nansen, "What is the Way?" "Ordinary mind, everyday life, is the Way," Nansen replied. "Shall I try to seek after it?" Joshu asked. "If you try for it, you will become separated from it," responded Nansen. "How can I know the Way unless I try for it?" persisted Joshu. Nansen said, "The Way is not a matter of knowing or not knowing. Knowing is delusion; not knowing is confusion. When you have really reached the true Way beyond doubt, you will find it vast and boundless. How can it be talked about on the level of right and wrong?" With these words, Joshu came to sudden realization."

These Boots Were Made for Walking

No one, in his right mind, would trek
from North China to South as young Joshu did
to find Master Nansen. I surmise this
studying the narratives at the Asian Art Museum
in San Francisco, standing amid stunning statues
of Buddhas—bronzed, wooden, clay.
China is mountainous, rivers running east
to west the main means of travel. To walk
from north to south, over treacherous gorges,
through snow, mired in mud, drenched in rain,
is to travel because you must: fleeing
a bandit's sword, an Emperor's whim,
or seeking enlightenment. The need to flee
ordinary mind must have been extraordinary,
for Joshu. Certainly I am committed enough to fight
San Francisco traffic, pay through the nose for parking,
find my way here, at the feet of these gorgeous,
serene, luminous Buddhas. But like Joshu,
I find their subtle Mona Lisa smiles maddening:
move towards it, you go away from it;
seeking, it escapes you; do nothing,
nothing happens. But I don't mind
the journey. Perhaps my very ordinary mind
will find itself trekking south to north,
Santa Cruz to San Francisco, and back again.
Every mud slide, broken bridge, traffic jam
a way of finding what is always
already *Here.*

Koan 20 — A Man of Great Strength

Master Shogen said, "Why is it that a man of great strength cannot lift his leg?" Again he said, "It is not with his tongue that he speaks."

When The Carnival Comes To Town

It's an odd circus hailing from old Asia,
trailers parked on the edge of this town called Mind,
the carny calling one and all to enter
the immense multi-colored big-top tent
of Mount Sumeru and the Scented Ocean.
Ticket in hand, you enter through the Zen curtains,
see Master Shogen in the center ring
with his bull-horn, shouting, *See
the strongest man alive who can't lift a finger!
Listen to the woman with no tongue speak!*
With your popcorn and lemonade,
you take a seat in the wooden folding chairs,
gaze at the immense mountain surrounded
by blue-green sea, and overhead at the top
a canopy of a beautiful woman's face
looking down from the heavens. Then
the grandmaster disappears. The bull-horn
lies on the dirt floor of the empty center ring.
But you sit awhile longer, waiting for anything.
Silence. Not one show in the big tent. Finally,
you notice a ladder spiraling up near the exit,
catch Master Shogen ascending the metal steps—
so you follow. One dizzying step after another
till finally you land on the scaffold at the top,
see Shogen gesturing towards a harness of
leather straps and metal buckles that dangles
you, weightless, over a canvas painted
front and back like heaven, with peep-holes
that are the eyes of the beautiful woman
in the tent ceiling. You surrender. Strap each leg
and arm in, useless in the open air, pull
yourself towards the peep holes till you

peer down, speechless, as the most beautiful woman in the world. The tent filled now, everyone clapping, especially you, still seated in that same wooden folding chair, riveted, unable to move one leg, utter a single word.

Koan 21 — Ummon's Shit-Stick

A monk asked Ummon, "What is Buddha?" Ummon said, "A shit-stick!"

In Case You Think This Is Metaphor

Until he had the flying dream,
as in, *being a fly,* the monk thought the koan
an exaggeration. Or simply a Master's trick.
But traveling in the wilderness,
using a stick to dig a hole
for the most pleasurable dump
he'd ever taken on a stony hillside,
he knew the Buddha must have had
many such moments. And the buzzing fly—
sensing only perfumed beauty
in the mysterious pile before its burial.
Ummon knew, too, the monk realized—
with every trip to the outhouse.
It is the literal body of the world,
this Buddha.

Koan 22 — Kasho and The Flagpole

Ananda once said to Kasho, "The World-Honored One gave you the golden robe; did he not give you anything else?" Kasho called out, "Ananda!" Ananda answered, "Yes, sir." Kasho said, "Knock down the flagpole at the gate."

Half-Mast Is Not Enough

Master Kasho was now old as the Buddha
would have been, if not for the bad mushrooms.
Ananda was the Buddha's nephew,
his constant attendant while he lived.
Could recite from memory every wisdom
so that listeners thought this brilliant,
luminous man was the Buddha returned.
A flag was hoisted on the pole of the
temple gate whenever a master spoke,
but Ananda always deferred to his uncle
or Master Kasho in his own mind,
still paced the turning halls of memory,
fussed over the scrolls of Buddha's sayings
with a mind sharp as a tiger hunting
for prey that still eluded him. Aging, desperate,
Ananda finally called to Master Kasho,
He gave it to you, the golden robe,
isn't there something else!

With one penetrating call of his own
Buddha name, *Ananda!,* Master Kasho shouted:
Knock down the whole god-damn flag pole!
And he became at once the flag, the pole,
the tiger, and the uncle.

KOAN 23 —THINK NEITHER GOOD NOR EVIL

Master Eno was once pursued by the Monk Myo as far as Taiyu Mountain. Seeing Myo coming, Master Eno laid the robe and bowl on a rock and said, "This robe represents the faith; it should not be fought over. If you want to take it away, take it now". Myo tried to move it, but it was as heavy as a mountain and would not budge. Faltering and trembling, he cried out, "I came for the Dharma, not for the robe. I beg you, please give me your instruction." Master Eno said, "Think neither good nor evil. At this very moment, what is the original self of the monk Myo?" At these words, Myo was illuminated. His whole body was covered with sweat. He wept and bowed, saying, "Besides the secret words and the secret meaning you have just now revealed to me, is there anything else, deeper still?" Master Eno said, "What I have told you is no secret at all. When you look into your own true self, whatever is deeper is found right there." Myo said, "I was with the monks under Obai for many years but could not realize my true self. But now, receiving your instruction, I know it is like a man drinking water and knowing whether it is cold or warm. My lay brother, you are now my teacher." Master Eno said, "If you are so awakened, both you and I have Obai as our teacher. Be mindful to treasure what you have attained."

Hide & Seek

Myo had been a general before becoming a monk
at Mt. Obai. He knew how to get things done.
And this young, illiterate layman, this Eno,
must have stolen the Master's robe, filched
his bowl—proofs of dharma transmission.
Thinking only a thief would run, Myo finally
cornered Eno on a mountain ridge after
weeks of tracking, demanded the return
of bowl and robe. Eno knew his old master
had called him in secret on that dark night
after composing the only poem in the Dharma
contest reflecting the Buddha's mind—
given him his treasures, told him to run, to hide,
till the senior, cultured monks could receive
such a master as he. When Myo saw Eno
place robe and bowl on the ground, say,
Please, take them... the former general was undone.
Everyone fights—especially at the monastery,
currying favor, defending doctrines, hoping
to become the next master. Eno was just himself,
open, transparent. Myo sweated. Wept. Bowed.
Asked for the secret, for something deeper
still. Eno said, *There is no secret, and it is
in you. There is no way to hide it!*

Myo awoke—but being an old general, knew
the world, and monks. Decided to live
on the mountain away from such intrigues for a time,
bid the young master goodbye. Eno continued
on his way, lived in hiding for ten years
as his master bid. Till appearing right on time
as we might, in koan twenty-nine.

KOAN 24 —WITHOUT WORDS, WITHOUT SILENCE

A monk once asked Master Fuketsu, "Without speaking, without silence, how can you express the truth?" Fuketsu observed, "I always remember the spring in southern China. The partridges are calling, and the flowers are fragrant."

Non-Sequitur

for John Tarrant

The only thing worse than speaking, John says,
is not saying anything. Poetry is a way
of not answering the world as though it were
a question, spring its own kind of awakening,
as is Texas, or Wall Street, even dead flowers,
fragrance floating among the folded blankets
of the brain, falling into the empty spaces
between letters.

Tasmania is a way of saying I come from a place
that is everywhere, John looking like that devil
in the skull, the Looney Tunes of the mind,
with our short tempers, little patience, appetites
that know no bounds. Like *Taz* in the cartoon,
he spins like a vortex, biting through any-thing.
Like Fuketsu, a partridge in his heart.
Words that smell of Sonoma.
A flower in his teeth.

Koan 25 —Talk by the Monk of the Third Seat

Master Gyozan had a dream: He went to Maitreya's place and was given the third seat. A venerable monk there struck the table with a gavel and announced, "Today the talk will be given by the monk of the third seat." Gyozan struck the table with the gavel and said, "The Dharma of Mahayana goes beyond the Four Propositions and transcends the One Hundred Negations. Listen carefully!"

NAKED AND DREAMING

Here it is again, the dream:
I'm in the third grade, sitting
in the third seat near the teacher,
naked as a blue jay, terrified she'll
call on me. Mrs. Maitreya looks
like an ancient Chinese Buddha
with her pearl hat, her kindly
hint of a smile, the way she stares
right through me as though I were,
well, naked. As though all of me,
the entire wrecked and embarrassing
world that I am, is the perfect answer
to the question she is about to ask.
She hits her desk with that big ruler
to garner the attention of the unruly
classroom, and sure enough
calls on me to stand next to her, recite
the poem I've just written.
The blank sheet of paper in my hand
is no help, but she just winks,
takes me by the shoulders, turns me
to look at thirty-three students
at their wooden desks, just as naked,
just as terrified. Commands me
to speak. Then I wake up.

KOAN 26 —TWO MONKS ROLL UP THE BAMBOO BLINDS

The monks gathered in the hall to hear the Great Hogen of Seiryo give teisho before the midday meal. Hogen pointed to the bamboo blinds. At this two monks went to the blinds and rolled them up alike. Hogen said, "One has it; the other has not."

Twins

*the One and the Many,
the Absolute and the Relative*

Born of the same mother, they loved each other,
did everything together. Even twins, though,

have their own ways: the first-born preferring
games that have no end, in which he could lose

himself; the second-born loving games he could
solve quickly, with a clear winner. Uncle Hogen

razzed them mercilessly when he visited.
His favorite game was called, *Roll up the blinds.*

He'd sit in the big easy chair with his feet up,
one twin under each arm, then shout, *Go!*

They'd race to the bay windows, grab a cord,
see who could roll the bamboo blinds up first

without jamming the twine or the slats. They
had to do this blindfolded. Uncle Hogen would

declare a winner, though half the time he'd
simply laugh, choose one of them randomly.

They couldn't tell the difference, nor did they mind.
As long as the elder got to play with his brother.

And the younger, obsessed with winning,
was happy to beat his older brother half the time.

Uncle Hogan? He was the luckiest man in the world,
no matter who won.

Koan 27 — Neither Mind Nor Buddha

A monk once asked Master Nansen, "Is there any Dharma that has not yet been taught to the people?" Nansen said, "Yes, there is." The monk asked, "What is the Dharma that has not been taught to the people?" Nansen said, "It is neither mind, nor Buddha, nor beings."

Monopoly

The Master loved playing Monopoly.
It reminded him of teaching Zen students.
There was no way they'd play unless
there was something to win. So he'd
lead them on, let them acquire properties,
monopolies, little green houses like meditation huts,
big hotels red as the royal monasteries of old.
Throw in a railroad or two to get somewhere
fast, or utilities to control the water and lights.
Of course, the point of the game
is that there's always another property
to acquire, hut to build, monastery to erect.
Enlightenment to get. The students
have to figure the secret out for themselves.
They wouldn't believe the old guy
if he told them there's no monopoly to get,
only this wandering around the board,
visiting each other, drinking tea at Park Place,
paying through the nose for dinner
and a clean bed at the Boardwalk.
Laughing about it the whole time.

Koan 28 — Ryutan Blows Out the Candle

Tokusan asked Ryutan about Zen far into the night. At last Ryutan said, "The night is late. Why don't you retire?" Tokusan made his bows and lifted the blinds to withdraw, but he was met by darkness. Turning back to Ryutan, he said, "It is dark outside." Ryutan lit a paper candle and handed it to him. Tokusan was about to take it when Ryutan blew it out. At this, all of a sudden, Tokusan went through a deep experience and made bows. Ryutan said, "What sort of realization do you have?" "From now on," said Tokusan, "I will not doubt the words of an old osho who is renowned everywhere under the sun."

The next day Ryutan ascended the rostrum and said, "I see a fellow among you. His fangs are like the sword tree. His mouth is like a blood bowl. Strike him with a stick, and he won't turn his head to look at you. Someday or other, he will climb the highest of the peaks and establish the Way there." Tokusan brought his notes on the *Diamond Sutra* to the front of the hall, pointed to them with a torch, and said, "Even though you have exhausted the abstruse doctrines, it is like placing a hair in a vast space. Even though you have learned all the secrets of the world, it is like a drop of water dripped on the great ocean." He burned all his notes. Then, making bows, took his leave of his teacher.

Waking to the Dark

It is dark outside, he said. *Then blow out the candle,*
she replied. It was the same each anniversary,
their banter a way of loving. His words, like fangs
or swords, long since quieted. Her words,
like a sharp stick to the head, no longer drawing blood.
They'd climb the peak each year with their tortured
journals, burn them page by page in a Tibetan
prayer bowl. Take one silver hair from the head
of the other, let it float down over the cliff
into vast space. Like a secret no one could trace.
The world is like this. Someone says, *It is dark outside,*
and another replies, *Then blow out the candle.*

Koan 29 — Neither the Wind Nor the Flag

The wind was flapping a temple flag. Two monks were arguing about it. One said the flag was moving; the other said the wind was moving. Arguing back and forth they could come to no agreement. The Sixth Ancestor Eno approached and said, "It is neither the wind nor the flag that is moving. It is your mind that is moving." The two monks were struck with awe.

Beyond The Eye

Eno whispers…a fish swims in water,
never knowing *ocean*. Burrowing, the worm is blind
to earth. Each bird assumes the air. For me,
there are hints: driving down the road,
everyone in front is too slow, everyone behind
too fast. The good that happens seems meant
to be; everything bad someone else's failure.
Secretly, I prefer the old cosmology, the universe
revolving round the earth, me at the center.
Or reading Darwin, I begin to believe:
all is survival, nothing is play. Others
are always better, always worse.

But then I notice flying squirrels that soar
between trees; how whales swim in one world,
breathe in another; and in Australia,
how aborigines move from *dreaming*
to here and back again. I once asked
a man who died, just for a moment,
what it was like. He'd felt himself floating
above the emergency room table
as his body completed its heart attack,
watched as he slipped back inside
the body's glove, opened his eyes.
Felt the *I* behind the eye—this mind
we move through without even seeing.

Koan 30 — This Very Mind is the Buddha

Daibai asked Baso, "What is the Buddha?" Baso answered, "This very mind is the Buddha."

Somewhere Over the Rainbow

Like Dorothy after the tornado, I crave
to leave this dusty farm of the mind behind,
the cows that moo unmercifully till milked,
these chicken-thoughts always clucking,
the pigs, well, just being pigs. If it took
a tornado, a whack on the head, I wouldn't
mind—if it brought bluebirds, clouds,
a yellow brick road, an Emerald City ruled
by the great bodhisattva Oz who could grant
what I most lacked: intelligence, courage,
a heart. But sometimes it takes a long journey
to discover: I am the witch, the tin man, the lion,
even the smart scarecrow with no brain,
arms pointing in all directions at once.
I might even be the Buddha behind the curtain,
handing me red shoes, a shovel, saying,
There's no place like home.

Koan 31 — Joshu Sees Through the Old Woman

A monk asked an old woman, "Which way should I take to Mount Gotai?" The old woman said, "Go straight on!" When the monk had taken a few steps, she remarked, "He may look like a fine monk, but he too goes off like that!" Later, the monk told Joshu about it. Joshu said, "Wait a while. I will go and see through that old woman for you." The next day he went, and asked her the same question. The old woman, too, gave him the same reply. When he returned, Joshu announced to the monks, "I have seen through the old woman of Mount Gotai for you."

City Slicker

I love the scene between Billy Crystal
and Jack Palance,
the city boy in midlife crisis terrified
of the grizzled cowboy who sees
right through him, might just as easily
shoot him as lead him down the right path.
Billy drones on about his neuroses,
oblivious to old Jack's impatience
with his nervous tics and flailings.
Cigarette dangling from his sun-wizened lips,
cowboy hat tilted back by leather-gloved hand,
Jack asks, *Do you know what the secret of life is?*
And Billy says, *No, what?* Jack lifts his finger
just like Gutei, and Billy of course mocks,
Your finger? Jack leans in, growls,
One thing, just one thing. You stick to that
and everything else don't mean shit,
which is sort of a Buddha thing to say.
Billy wants to know what the *One Thing*
is, eyes open, longing. Like Jack,
the old weathered sages with their red
cowboy scarves just crack a wry smile,
point you

down the one and only path
you can ever walk.

Note Master Gutei's "one finger Zen" in Koan Number Three

Koan 32 — Questioning the Buddha

A non-Buddhist philosopher once asked the Buddha, "I do not ask for words, nor do I ask for no-words." The Buddha remained seated. The philosopher said admiringly, "The Buddha, with his great mercy, has blown away the clouds of my illusion and enabled me to enter the Way." After making bows, he took his leave. Then Ananda asked the Buddha, "What did he realize, to admire you so much?" The Buddha replied, "A fine horse runs even at the shadow of the whip."

Be Careful What You Ask For

The Brahmin sage was tired of debate. *Always*,
he thought, the mind fails—mired
time and again in opposing points of view.
Philosophy is a tough business—materialism,
idealism, one hundred positions between.
The difference between a lawyer and a sage
increasingly blurry. But this Buddha
doesn't bow to the bridle of my question.
And those eyes—like a thousand answers
to a question I've never asked.
A kind of horse-sense—inviting me to run
in the shadows where nothing is known
except hoof-fall and cloud, oat and apple,
hint of the wind's whip.

Koan 33 — No Mind, No Buddha

A monk asked Baso, "What is the Buddha?" Baso answered, "No mind, no Buddha."

Bargaining

Master Baso is like a tough vendor
in the marketplace, haggling
over the price of mushrooms, knives,
meat. You know you both want a sale,
that's not the question. The aroma
of blue-fish, ginger and red pepper,
a silky blade to prepare them with—
all are too seductive to resist. But
one thing Baso never budges on:
No mind, no Buddha. No meal
without the body, no feast
without hunger, no enlightenment
without the knife to slice it open.

Koan 34 — Mind Is Not the Way

Nansen said, "Mind is not the Buddha; reason is not the Way."

Treasure Map

The pirate Nansen pointed to the blood-red "X"
on the map, where the treasure lay. Buried
ten thousand nautical leagues from here,
many fathoms deep. I squinted my eyelids
at the weathered parchment, sighed. It
seemed a catastrophic distance for my
greedy sailor heart, but I desperately
craved the minted gold, the rubies,
a king's chalice, a jade Buddha
from the Orient. Pirate Nansen
chuckled, *Move over there boy,*
you're looking at it all wrong.
With one wave of his ruffled
black and burgundy sleeve,
he grasped the old map
in both grizzled hands,
swiveled it sideways,
gleamed a wry smile
and a golden tooth,
whispered, *X marks*
the spot you're on,
lad. Your treasure
is straight down
at the bottom
of your
sea.

KOAN 35 — SEIJO'S SOUL SEPARATED

Goso said to his monks, "Seijo's soul separated from her being. Which was the real Seijo?"

The One Seijo

She'd been promised to Osho as a child,
though her father had forgotten,
planned to wed her to another.
Heartbroken, Seijo fell sick
as Osho fled the village, though
he found her running in the dark
along the shore just as he set sail
in his small boat at midnight. They fled
together, bore children, loved deeply.
But the world was not aligned, each
missed their families intensely.
One day, they knew it was time,
and sailed home. Osho found
her father, told him their story,
that Seijo awaited his blessing
at the harbor to return home.
But the father, astonished, said
she had been bed-ridden for years,
was still inside his home.

When Osho fetched Seijo from the harbor,
and her father fetched Seijo from her bed,
the two women met and became one.
I myself am not sure which is the real me,
the one Seijo whispered.

Note: From "Rikon-ki" – The Story of the Separated Soul

KOAN 36 — WHEN YOU MEET A MAN OF THE WAY

Goso said, "When you meet a man of the Way on the path, do not meet him with words or with silence. Tell me, how then will you meet him?"

Best Friends

The back porch at night is alight
with falling meteors, radiance
a million years deep—that's
how long it takes for some light
to reach here, for some words
to come. After awhile, cigars lit,
whisky poured, there's not even
much to say. You whistle that
old tune of Dharma, *She'll be
coming round the mountain
when she comes...* You peer
wistfully into the ambient abyss.
A sip to keep you warm.
Smoke to make things clear.

KOAN 37 — JOSHU'S OAK TREE

A monk asked Joshu, "What is the meaning of Bodhidharma's coming to China?" Joshu said, "The oak tree in the garden."

Straight Talk

Joshu thought these monks so earnest,
mustering the courage to ask, again,
the one question considered the essence
of Zen. They often looked crestfallen
when he looked about for whatever
was handy, said, *The oak tree in the garden;*
or, *The moon in the pond;* or dirt,
a grasshopper, a broken axe. They
wanted an answer so unimaginable,
so subtle, it would release their miserable
minds from prison, their befuddled hearts
from the outhouse. But Joshu knew
that Bodhidharma had not sailed all the way
from India with his tattoos, bug eyes,
bushy beard to just bring a new religion.
That was easy, and dull. Icons, beliefs,
scriptures. A true Zen master would
never handle a philosophical question
directly—the answer would be like
giving birth to a still-born ox. Better
to rip the outhouse door off its hinges,
pummel the prison-stone with a hammer,
peer into the pupils of each earnest monk.
Then look with them, hope they see the oak,
feel the Buddha's feet in their own,
this sun on arm and branch,
the partridge singing in the ear.

Koan 38 —An Ox Passes the Window

Goso said, "An ox passes by the window. His head, horns, and four legs all go past. But why can't the tail pass too?"

Ox-Tail Mind

This tail is a monster, said one master, *a world.*
The universe with its horny head,
matted hair, massive legs ambles by—
but this flicking tail is impossible
to grasp. Try to grab hold, come away with
busted knuckles, black eye, bleeding lip.
Better to sit, peer into this ocular
mirror, feel the tail
wag your body whole.

Koan 39 — You Have Missed It

A monk wanted to ask Ummon a question and started to say, "The light serenely shines over the whole universe…" Before he had even finished the first line, Ummon suddenly interrupted, "Isn't that the poem of Chosetsu Shusai?" The monk answered, "Yes, it is." Ummon said, "You have missed it!" Later, Master Shishin took up this koan and said, "Now tell me, why has this monk missed it?"

The Impersonator

He'd spent years practicing
in front of a mirror, arching eyebrows
like Jack Nicholson, frozen upper lip
of Humphrey Bogart, strong cadence
of John Wayne. Even Mae West's
husky voice, Dolly Parton's verve,
Hillary's presidential resolve.
Now, he could be anyone,
given enough time—recite
entire scripts, famous speeches,
hilarious jokes. The one person
that escaped him was himself.
So he took up Zen, became a poet.
Donned a black robe, a black
turtle-neck sweater, or both.
Memorized koans, poems,
the way his teachers sat: folded
legs in full lotus, blossoming.
The more he disciplined
his body, his tongue, his mind
to perfectly reflect the light,
the darker he felt. Till finally,
broken and empty, he gave up
being someone else. Then
John's bravado, Jack's eyebrow,
Mae's smile – and the Zen Master's
too – became him—the real deal,
the genuine article, his original face
before trying so damned hard.

KOAN 40 —TIPPING OVER A WATER PITCHER

When Master Isan was studying under Hyakujo, he worked as the cook at the monastery. Hyakujo wanted to choose an abbot for Daii Monastery. He told the head monk and all the rest of his disciples to make their Zen presentations, and the ablest one would be sent to found the monastery. Then Hyakujo took a pitcher, placed it on the floor, and asked the question: "This must not be called a pitcher. What do you call it?" The head monk said, "It cannot be called a wooden sandal." Hyakujo then asked Isan. Isan walked up, kicked over the pitcher, and left. Hyakujo said, "The head monk has been defeated by Isan." So Isan was ordered to start the new monastery.

CHARADES

Isan liked the charades his master played,
but years ago learned not to guess
what he was aiming at. No matter
what answer the other monks gave,
it was usually wrong, even if
it seemed true. The master
was after something truer,
so Isan kept watching, kept playing.
The years passed, and finally the master
needed to choose another master,
decided to play one more charade.
He set a water pitcher squarely on the floor
in front of all the monks, said,
Without using its name, what is it?!
The head monk had planned his answer
all morning, to say what it is not:
Well, it's not a sandal!
The master smiled, thought, *Clever...*
looked over at Isan and shrugged.
By now, Isan'd had enough, smiled back,
kicked the bottle over with his foot

as he walked out—clear water pooling
in the middle of the monastery floor
truer than any word, sweeter than any name.

Koan 41 — Bodhidharma and Peace of Mind

Bodhidharma sat in zazen facing the wall. The Second Patriarch, who had been standing in the snow, cut off his arm and said, "Your disciple's mind is not yet at peace. I beg you, my teacher, please give it peace." Bodhidharma said, "Bring the mind to me, and I will set it at rest." The Second Patriarch said, "I have searched for the mind, and it is unattainable." Bodhidharma said, "I have thoroughly set it at rest for you."

Zen Boot Camp

The snow was falling again, waist deep.
Had he really cut off his arm
to impress the master? His mind
was blurry as the winter storm
blowing snowflakes in flurries,
blinding his eyes, icing his thoughts
till all was frozen. Still, the master sat
facing the wall. Unmoving. As the hours
froze into days, he felt himself offer
first his toes, then his feet, his big ankles,
each shin, kneecap, thick thighs,
his shrinking genitals, sinking belly,
stubborn heart, now his arms
to the storm, to the master—unable,
to tell them apart. Even his mind
was gone. Everything offered,
even his lips, his skull.
The master finally opened
his eyes, led him inside to sit
by the fire. Now they could begin—
mind ungraspable as the storm
still blowing outside. His toes again
wriggling, his arm back in its socket,
lifting the iron kettle for tea.

Koan 42 — A Woman Comes Out of Meditation

Once long ago, the Buddha came to a place where many Buddhas were assembled. When Manjusri arrived, the Buddhas all returned to their original places. Only a woman remained, close to the Buddha seat in deep meditation. Manjusri spoke to the Buddha, "Why can a woman be close to the Buddha seat, and I cannot?" The Buddha told Manjusri, "You awaken this woman from her meditation and ask her yourself." Manjusri walked around the woman three times, snapped his fingers once, then took her up to the Brahma Heaven and tried all his supernatural powers, but he was unable to bring her out of meditation. The Buddha said, "Even hundreds of thousands of Manjusris would be unable to bring her out of meditation. Down below, past countries innumerable as the sands of the Ganges, there is a Bodhisattva called Momyo. He will be able to awaken her from meditation." In an instant Momyo emerged from the earth and worshiped the Buddha. The Buddha gave him the order. Momyo then walked to the woman and snapped his fingers only once. At this the woman came out of her meditation.

All I Really Need to Know I Learned in Kindergarten

The young woman went on a road trip
after graduating with a doctorate
to visit her old kindergarten teacher,
Mz. Momyo, with whom her long journey
had begun eons ago. Oh sure, it had been
grand, receiving her diploma from the hand
of Professor Manjusri, that wise and worldly
mentor to so many students. The president
himself had been the commencement speaker,
flanked by brilliant scientists, lawyers, poets,
economists, historians from the prestigious
university she'd attended. But she knew,
in her gut, what the latest research had shown:
more people remember their kindergarten
teacher than who discovered the atom or Pluto,
invented the wheel, toasters, mathematics.
Mz. Momyo had been the first to peer into
her eyes, light her lamp of curiosity, let her
color outside or inside the lines, turn books
upside down and make up different stories.
So when the young woman parked at the old
cement building that afternoon, walked into
the empty classroom after school, saw
Mz. Momyo look up from the stack
of brilliant chalk etchings that her latest
brood had produced, they both laughed—
snapped their fingers, just like old times, saying,
Are you awake today, my fine genius, are you awake?

Koan 43 — Shuzan and a Staff

Master Shuzan held up his staff, and showing it to the assembled disciples said, "You monks, if you call this a staff, you are committed to the name. If you call it not-a-staff, you negate the fact. Tell me, you monks, what do you call it?"

A Rose by Any Other Name

The *shippei* is made from a split piece of bamboo,
half a meter long, bound with wisteria vine
then lacquered. The symbol of a Zen master's
authority, it may be decorated with a silk cord,
elaborate carvings—is sometimes used
to rouse sleeping monks awake. It is also
a rose—yellow, pink, blood red, sometimes
orange or peach. A thorn is also its name,
dagger to open your calloused thumb,
your impenetrable heart. The sound it makes
winging towards slouching shoulder is like
the wind of dragons, its touch soft as
the lover who has waited several moons
for your return. Such a staff is the spine
rooting tailbone to skull, the Milky Way
whirling through the dark enigma of the void.
Call it by name, or let your lips fall silent,
it does not matter. Only that you grasp
what cannot be held with your whole body.
Whisper in its nameless ear something
of love—your original name, when the womb
was a temple, and you rushed through its doors
shouting.

Koan 44 — Basho and a Stick

Master Basho said to the monks, "If you have a stick, I shall give one to you. If you do not have a stick, I shall take it away from you."

Shtick

Whatever my gimmick,
Master Basho wants to take it away.
Even my *poor me* emptiness.
Especially this. The universe hands itself over
each moment—though half the time
I turn away, let it fall to the floor.
Or like a kid playing *Pick Up Sticks,*
I pry and prod to take just the right ones,
ignore the rest. Occasionally I manage
to pick up the fluorescent enlightenment
stick, phosphorescent pink or purple—
but when I start waving it dangerously,
he takes it away and everyone
is safe again. Master Basho
is like a mischievous ghost
peering through the eyes
and reaching through the hands
of those I meet. Giving me things,
taking them away. Ennui, hubris,
center stage, wallflower status.
Whatever my shtick, he bellows, *Hand it over!*
Till I laugh with him empty handed,
arms like tree branches before the carpenter
makes them useful.

Koan 45 —Who is He?

Hoen of Tozan said, "Even Shakyamuni and Maitreya are servants of another. I want to ask you, who is he?"

Missing Person

In the dream, I blink over my coffee cup
at the "missing children" pictures on the side
of the milk carton. Open the newspaper
to the Want-Ads, scan scores of personals
looking for the perfect mate, the hot date,
the discreet affair, enduring commitment.
For days on end I roam from one Post Office
to another, scan the "most-wanted"
on the bulletin board. Uncertain who it is
I am searching for. On the Internet,
I query, *Where is he now?* Find images,
clues—a god, bandits, saviors, thieves.
Still dreaming, Nietzsche points his finger
at me and yells, *Superman!* Jesus takes my hands,
turns them palm up, stares at the holes.
Freud calls me oceanic, Jung insists I am
all archetypes in one, Lao Tzu, that I am wind.
Krishna that I have a little golden *atman*
inside my heart. And Buddha simply
arches one eyebrow, looks at me expectantly.
Then I wake up. Stare into the bathroom mirror.

Koan 46 — Step Forward From the Top of a Pole

Master Sekiso said, "From the top of a pole one hundred feet high, how do you step forward?" An ancient Master also said that one sitting at the top of a pole one hundred feet high, even if he has attained 'it', has not yet been truly enlightened. He must step forward from the top of the pole one hundred feet high and manifest his whole body in the ten directions.

Mud Zen

I love the view at the top—
Half-Dome in Yosemite, immense granite
towering above the tiny redwoods in the valley.
The Empire State building's terraced roof;
asphalt streets, the cacophony of cabs far below.
I've heard the upper one percent of the upper
one percent have so much money
it almost becomes meaningless,
like the endless blue atop Mount Everest,
the rest of the world so far away you can't
touch it. I like the meditation joke about
the seeker who finally manages, after so much,
to attain the peak, finds the yogi sitting serenely
amid pure snow, white clouds, unimpeded views,
sits down and waits for *it* to happen—enlightenment,
all the rest. After a while, the yogi opens an eye,
looks over at the eager aspirant, finally says,
This is it. Everything else is happening down there.
The top of the pole is a tiny platform from which
to gaze at the world. Every day, my three-year-old
mind calls to me from the mud with a blueberry
stained face, wants me to make dark pies
in the earth's body.

Koan 47 — Tototsu's Three Barriers

Master Juetsu of Tosotsu made three barriers to test monks:

Inquiring after the Truth, groping your way through the underbrush, is for the purpose of seeing into your nature. Here, now, where is your nature?

If you realize your own nature, you are free from life and death. When your eyes are closed, how can you be free from life and death?

If you are free from life and death, you know where you will go. When the four elements are decomposed, where do you go?

Three Gates

The first gate creaks on rusted hinges, shrill
as the ghosts you've buried behind the decrepit
fence. On hands and knees, in rain, you fumble
through the underbrush for your life. But even
your silver tool cannot clear such rawness.
Then one day you wake in a garden of earth-
worms, creeping vines, wildflowers—heart
happy as a gopher tunneling the loamy soil,
nibbling roots sweeter than any flower.

The second gate you can only find with eyes
closed. The blind, here, have an advantage.
Intimacy is better up close, hand grasping
the invisible latch, feet feeling their way
barefoot on the stone path, toes burrowing
into mud near the spring where death and life
are the same fertile ground.

The third gate is, of course, the same
as the first two. There is only one life.
One way out. One way in. *Earth* as body,
wind to carry, *water* to nourish, *fire* to cook
the billion seeds of innumerable Buddhas.
It is a wide gate we pass through. No
one can miss it.

Koan 48 — Kempo's One Road

A monk said to Kempo Osho, "It is written, 'Bhagavats in the ten directions. One road to Nirvana.' I still wonder where the road can be." Kempo lifted his staff, drew a line, and said, "Here it is." Later the monks asked the same question of Ummon, who held up his fan and said, "This fan jumps up to the thirty-third heaven and hits the nose of the deity Sakra Devanam Indra. When you strike the carp of the eastern sea, the rain comes down in torrents."

ONE ROAD

Ummon thought, *You can tell them
over and over, but it does no good!*
Seekers in the ten directions,
running about like monks
who've lost their heads. Osho
kept it simple, drew a line
in the dirt right in front of them.
How much clearer can this be?
It's a hard road to miss, impossible
to veer from. The path emerges
right beneath each foot whether
you crawl, cavort, run, meander,
walk blind or plot each turn
on a detailed map. I've found
most like elaborate journeys,
someone else's treasure. That's
why I tell these bizarre tales:
my royal fan ascending
to the thirty-third heaven, hitting
Indra on the nose! Or striking
the great carp-headed dragon lying
in the stormy sea of the heart.
Then drowning in rain.
Eventually they tire of the dramatics,
sit still, stare at the ground.

Finally see the line in the dirt
impossible to miss, the one
they've been following all along.

Polishing the Moon Sword

Polishing the Moon Sword

On the eve of a decisive battle, Zhang Liang climbs Mount Ji Ming, played songs of the enemy soldiers' distant homeland. The soldiers become so nostalgic that most of them wander off, one by one, into the night. I see him still, in the Japanese print, purple robe flowing on cliff's edge, carved flute pressed to wet lips, unused sword quiet in the golden scabbard hanging from hip. His enigmatic heart happy for one less battle under the fierce moon.

A Good Death

Li Po has nothing to lose as he stares at the moon on the water. He is old, his body but a worn veil, though still hiding the Emperor's sword, given after a drunken bout of court poetry. Doing nothing—*wu-wei*—had been much harder than it seemed: escaping fame, escaping imperial princes after gambling, escaping the women who loved him. It was the moon he was devoted to, shimmering like a courtesan in poem after poem; or an old woman with no teeth, perhaps his mother, long dead. Or his first love, still mysterious. Once again, here she is on the night lake, teasing…*are you drunk again? Do you have another love? Can you still get it up, old poet?* They say he falls, drunk, out of his small boat and drowns trying to embrace the moon. But this time, after years of banter, perhaps he simply answers her, once and for all, with his whole useless body.

MICHIZANE COMPOSES A POEM BY MOONLIGHT

—Sugawara no Michizane (845-903)

After his death, he became the god of music, literature, calligraphy—titles an emperor may confer. But tonight, he is only eleven, composing a poem by moonlight. Moon of bright snow, moon of plum blossoms, moon of the golden mirror. Perhaps every young boy is a god. Every young heart a plum. Court life, accolades, love—all come later. For now, he is a poem: the curve of his slender arm the brush, his dark eyes the ink, his body caught somewhere between moonlight and dirt.

The Moon of the Milky Way

Shokiyo, the Weaver Maiden, fell so in love with Kengi the Herdsman, they both forgot their duties as constellations in the night sky. The Milky Way began to wander this way and that, stars like threads unraveling, stars like wild oxen scattering. This is one kind of loving. But Shokiyo's father worried his daughter would let the blanket of sky tatter to nothing, that Kengi would allow every star of heaven to stray from night's fence. This is the dark side of loving. So the father forbade the lovers to see each other except in the seventh month of each year, though he gave them the moon. This is another way of loving. The Milky Way again spiraling through the heavens like silver thread—a thousand glimmering beasts circling their one love.

Tsunenobu and the Demon

Watching the autumn moon rise, Tsunenobu hears the sound of cloth being pounded in the distance. He feels less alone now in the immense court where everyone else is sleeping, pulls his cold robe round him snugly. His demons, for a moment, are quiet. Remembering a famous poem, he whispers, *I listen to the sound of cloth being pounded as the moon shines serenely…here is someone else who has not yet gone to sleep.* Suddenly, a gigantic demon appears in the sky, the one he most fears. It, too, recites a poem: *In the northern sky, geese fly across the Big Dipper; to the south, cold robes are pounded under the moonlight.* Tsunenobu laughs — for no one likes to be alone under an autumn moon. Least of all your demon.

Tzu Yu's Lament

The four old men look at each other and laugh, *Who can make non-being their head, life their spine, death their butt—all one body—these are true friends!* Before long, of course, one of them becomes ill. When the others visit, he says, *It's amazing! The Dark Enigma is crumpling me into such an embrace: a hunched back, chin tucked into belly, shoulders topping skull, nape pointed at sky.* Hobbling over to a well, he looks at himself in the water, sighs again, *Such an embrace.* All four friends know where they are headed. Her strong arms, silken skin, welcome them one by one. Like a mother, folding them shoulder by hip back into her body.

Cloth-Beating Moon

Her orange kimono draped round her pale shoulders, she raises the wooden mallet, pounds robe after robe smooth on the wooden block under a pale moon. Hoping her husband will hear in the distance, wherever he may be. The steady percussion a kind of music or poem. It's melancholy drifting through the villages, echoing in the hills. Her long black hair tangled, her nails broken, the palms of her hands calloused. Her orange kimono immaculate. Each night. While her husband, the war finally over, lifts his bruised head, hears the steady, muffled sound of his wife pounding cloth. Follows the pale moon home.

Return to Moon Palace

An old bamboo basket maker and his childless wife adopt an abandoned baby girl, name her *Kaguyahime*, radiant beauty, like the world. As she reaches the age for marrying, many suitors, including the emperor, seek her hand. It is only now, when someone seeks to keep her, that she reveals herself as daughter of Joga, Queen of the Moon. Her parents hide her away, the emperor sends emissaries to bring her to the palace. But she can never be held by anyone, and returns to the night heavens. Each evening, the emperor is haunted, but the old bamboo cutter and his wife kneel in the dirt, turn their wrinkled faces toward the moon, whisper, *I see you.* Watch her gray kimono, white face, ebony hair appear and disappear.

Mount Miyagi Moon

His brown kimono, long dark hair over broad shoulders, fine beard gracing a strong chest, are all of one piece. Bittersweet. Like the melancholy tune he plays on his lute in the forest. Marooned on this island after a failed rebellion, a man's fortunes may turn on one arrow, one captured letter, a single wrong turn. Longing for home, he plays. Each string plucked quivers the moon in its slivered light through the leaves. The mountain, like his grief, is immoveable. Though this moon, too, will wane, this song become a boat to return him home.

Moon of the Red Cliffs

The full moon is alight over the Red Cliffs of the Yangtze River. The poet Su Shi tires of his scholar friends, and the artists, rhapsodizing over a famous battle eight centuries earlier—here, under this same moon. *One must know a sword as a sword to write of a sword*, he huffs, *know blood red on its moonlit tip*. Eyeing his friends in the long boat, Su Shi oars them silently beneath the hulking cliffs, takes the knife hidden in his sleeve, wounds the thumb of each—bids them to write a poem in their own blood. Only then do scholar and painter and poet see the dead under the cliffs.

BLIND MOON

The blind warrior, *Taira no Tomoume*, fights with the talisman of a poem on his back. Now, as in the twelfth century, the world blindsides. My mind, also. A sword can only protect so much. Taira's verse, *From darkness I have wandered, lost to even a darker path*, is my own. But there is the clouded light of this heart. His poem between my shoulder blades. A stone underfoot. A blind moon ahead.

Lonely Moon

Li Chi, the most beautiful woman in China, walks to the pond edge, sees carp scurry into deeper water. Then, lounging under the cherry blossom tree, she sees birds escape into azure sky. She wanders into the forest, spies deer scampering away. Even men in the village are afraid, turn their faces.

New Moon Grief

The poor fisherman understands. The general rummages among the reeds of the Huai River after the war, looking for the grave of the emperor who'd taken his brother and father in battle. Thinking of his own son, the fisherman guides the general through bamboo, mist, darkness. Finds the hasty tomb. Steals the dead emperor's body, whips it three hundred times beneath the dark moon.

Mad Moon

Ochiyo, the young maidservant, runs into the streets of the capital with her dead lover's rolled parchment letters. Rolling and unrolling them into tatters. He was the only one who'd recognized her heart. Whispered its name. Made love with his eyes. Kept her secret. To be seen, then abandoned—this is only the beginning of grief's long unrolling. Some say she died that day. Others, that she roams the alleys of their hearts still, her yellow kimono shining like a feral moon.

Poem of the Body

Fujiwara falls asleep on the veranda of the Shinto shrine devoted to the patron deity of poets. It has been a long journey here from the palace. One sandal broken, feet muddy, heart troubled. His poems like still-born birds, unable to fly from the egg. Why are his verses filled with dead blossoms, rain that will not fall, lovers that do not kiss? Perhaps here, at the shrine, single stick of incense smoking in the rice bowl, the *kami* of poetry will find him. Make life in the palace possible again. Instead, he falls asleep—and in his dream, the ghost of the old man he'd soon enough become frowns. Dips an ink brush in the mud, writes a single *kanji* character on the sole of each foot, one for the belly, the heart, each shoulder and knee. Thus he becomes the poem he seeks.

Moon of the Filial Son

His bare feet feel good on the cool earth. Hands bind sticks in a bundle for his aging parents' fire. In the morning the imperial court will need him, renowned for his calligraphy and poems. To be so esteemed for inked brush strokes—partridge, frog, peony blossoms in verse the emperor prizes to keep the kingdom in harmony – it is an honor. But tonight, he wears the ragged kimono given by his father, mended by his mother—grateful for the waning light of each cratered moon face.

Wolf Moon Musician

His imperial green kimono, black top hat, are no protection from the wolves on the moors north of Kyoto, where he wanders at night. Not even the emperor, in whose court he plays, can command the wolves. Nor the mind—a fickle beast in the dark. Grief like fangs, like yellow eyes. Lips on wooden flute, he plays the mournful tune the emperor hates, but the wolves love. It is his own tune. Under the clouded moon he becomes tooth and tongue and wild.

Fisticuffs

After Lao Tzu dies, his friend Chi'in Shih strides into the burial grounds and shouts three times. His eyes red and wet. Chin trembling, legs like fallen stone. The other followers are stoic, like storm hiding in cloud. Lao Tzu had said, *hiding from heaven* is the only crime—so Chi'in Shih raises his arms skyward, shakes his fists. Makes sure his friend can see.

Getting Free of the Gods

The old hunchback sighs as he settles bamboo cane against the blackened hearth. He welcomed the gods, most of his life. It was the only way to be free of them. To be so at home in this crooked world, even *T'ien – Fate* is greeted at the door. Given a stool by the fire, a table to display the jade knife, the emerald vial of perfume and poison.

The Moon's Four Strings

Semimaru tunes the strings of his lute under the full moon. Blind, of noble birth, his poetry falls upon the ears of listeners like cherry blossoms floating down towards death. The melancholy of his four strings opens the chest, lets in the moon. Tonight, he plays alone in his mountain cottage near Kyoto. Yet somehow, centuries later, I hear him still. This same moon, tuning the heart like a lute.

Exile

Nine dragons tattoo his body—flame from each hand and foot, the belly with its fanged grimace, the chest dragon's fiery mouth, each shoulder a dragon wing, the ninth secreted, never revealed. Whether *Shi Jin* is an outlaw depends on the dark ink's bleed. Rulers fear his dragon-skin, neighbors welcome his stealth—leaving here a coin, there an egg. Ink is stronger than sword. Those with nothing know: dragons lurk in the body. Wake when hunted.

Cassia Tree Moon

Wu Gang stands in the Japanese print, immense axe with red sun scabbard in one fist, the other pointing toward a moon filling half the page. Blue robe tousled, black beard scraggly from neglect. Legend says he wanted too much—condemned by the gods to forever chop the branches of eight magical cassia trees on the moon, which simply grow again when axed. He does not look unhappy. What better prison could there be? Walls of night, this immense light. He sharpens the iron blade, aims again at the root, hoping his sentence might last forever.

The Broken Water Bucket

Lady Chiyo fills the old bucket from the river as she's done for years. Even a celebrated poet must carry her own water, particularly among men. But tonight, finally, the bottom of the bucket gives way, and the river she's carried all her life spills over moss and dirt. The moon, however, still glows in each tiny pooled lake beneath her feet.

Eclipse Moon of Lady Iga

Her long black hair, like the dark moon, holds many ghosts. At court, all is hidden beneath white powder, red rouge, the cascade of hair bound in whorled bun. Old loves, emperors, demons—her many selves threaten suicide by knife in the courtyard of the heart. But each night, serenely, she lets down her dark river of hair, bids each ghost swim in her numinous light, nothing eclipsed.

Traveling Together

Old P'ang sells bamboo baskets with his daughter for food while traveling. They have less than the deer in the forest, the gophers underground—no shame in this. Bamboo is plentiful, his gnarled hands rich with the skill to bend, to shape. Knobby knees cause him to stumble, bruise his wrinkled face in the dirt. Ling-chao, his daughter, throws herself on the ground beside him, stares into his eyes. Always, he cries, *What are you doing?* Each time, she smiles mischievously, *I'm helping!*

Five Beauties

The unknown women on the hanging silk scroll are intent—white faces powdered, lips rouged, black hair pinned with lacquered wood spools, red ribbon. One feathers a poem on long parchment, another inks dark trees under moon, a third plucks the strings of the *koto*, two recline in intimate conversation. In the pleasure quarters, there are many heavens, many hells. Who can know the heart? Whether the black ink sings or mourns, the strings lament, which moon-face secretly loves, which is running away among the smudged, blurry trees.

Famous Places

The parchment is ground with gold paint, entitled *Famous Places of Kyoto*. A samurai watches dancers with yellow fans, a red-robed child points toward the whirring kimonos, while the scene on the ground floor is filled with beggars, merchants, a farmer sipping tea in a shop, a lady carried by two men naked but for striped loincloth. A hawker in white knee-length robe waves a white fan toward the elevated second story where the samurai sits impassive, still watching. Art is an eye. Even the dirt is mottled with gold.

Thirty-Six Poets

In Hoitsu's painting, the middle poet rests chin on palm—ironic eyes, petulant mouth beneath fine-lined mustache, itself a poem. That fame is hollow, perhaps, or the bald-headed monk adjacent too spiritual, the drunken fat man beneath just lucky? A shy woman in the corner hides behind her hair, while the old woman at the top whispers a wry joke to the buffoon with folded fan. Their kimonos shimmer for a moment. Though the middle poet, I can tell, is unsure anyone will remember.

The Forests of Mount Fuji

Takeda Shingen sits in flame red robe contemplating the impenetrable forest at the foot of Mount Fuji—the inaccessible sea, his prize, beyond. Helmet of snow white hair falling over broad shoulders, horned antler fixed atop his brow, he ponders the bitterness of failure. Thoughts like his army, entangled by the roadless forest, the hidden enemy. His landlocked province defeated by the very mountain worshiped. Perhaps the girth of dream is enough. Mount Fuji his Muse, more steady than the feckless sea.

Moon of the Vengeful Ghosts

The warrior-priest Benkei stands in the prow of his proud boat, exorcising demons. Immense black waves, conjured by dead enemies, threaten to engulf his boat, kill his men, grieve their families. In the Kabuki plays, Benkei is able, sometimes, to calm the ghosts, row unharmed to shore. Other nights, he drowns beneath moonlight streaking the black waves silver. Tonight, the taste of salt in mouth as he conjures, he wonders which way the play will turn—if prayers will tame the dark mountains of water, the ghost moon drown or calm his hurricane heart.

Abandoned Old Woman

Her son's broad back is strong as it carries her frail body up the mountain. The poorer families do this, she bears no ill will for her eldest. Wonders only who will carry him up this same mountain when his bones clatter like a broken rattle. The bent pine near the crest is what she motions her stoic son to lay her against, to see the moon rise one last night, or two, over the village she bore him in. No regret, this death. Gnarled trunk of pine and woman, this pale moon rising.

Old Nurse

The moment Saito, now a samurai, creaked the broken gate, slid back the rice paper door, she knew he was hunted. The failed attack on the cruel warlord, the flight through night and swamp ghosts, the eyes of spies, the single arrow or silver blade that would soon be his fate. Parents dead, it was she, invisible as the new moon, he returned to. Kimono laid aside, dirty sandals left outside, she bathed his brow, his wounds, his neck one last time—holding him as the gift he was when first they placed him against her breast. Her body his alone.

Koan Moon

After his death, Zi Luo will be revered as one of the Twenty-Four Paragons of Filial Piety for tending his parents in old age. Tonight, he is merely a middle-aged man with graying beard who carries a heavy sack of rice to them. His eyes squint under the full moon, reading an ancient text as he walks. They'd been poor till he learned poetry, the ways of government, became a scholar. Often, the moon is his only light for reading while carrying wood for father, smoothing his mother's white hair. The days too burdened for study. But sometimes, the moon shines bright enough for his tired eyes to see the inked *koan* his mind can never solve the riddle of. Though his blind feet never fail to find the stony path.

Lucky Moon

Hotei, one of the Seven Lucky Gods, points his stubby finger toward a full, white moon. Fat legged, rotund, he rests his formidable body against the immense bag of treasure he carries. Inside, most assume there is jade, gold—worship this god of good fortune. Wish for happiness. Hotei, always amused, laughs again. If only they knew: his canvas bag, like his body, is filled with all he has been. Like the moon, carved by dark into slivers, illuminated again with secret light. His stubby finger points even when the moon is empty, his bag empty, his life empty. How else to instruct crazed followers, who ransack his bag, throw most things away, curse the emptiness. His fingers point still toward light in the dark sky, his tongue wagging, *Lucky Hotei! Lucky Hotei!* The moon waning, the moon waxing.

Acknowledgments

A special note of appreciation to two of my poetic teachers in this endeavor. John Tarrant, director and roshi of The Pacific Zen Institute in Santa Rosa, California, first introduced me to this way of working with traditional Zen koans. As a poet himself, as well as a former Jungian therapist, he brings incredible depth and creativity to re-imagining koan-work in the West. I'm grateful for his vision, big Tasmanian heart, sailing skills, and his poetry.

Gary Young, esteemed poet, print-maker, and lecturer at the University of California, Santa Cruz, and First poet Laureate of Santa Cruz, California, is a master of the prose poem, whose work is published in an array of books, periodicals, broadsides, housed in private collections and museums.

I thank Poetry Santa Cruz, for unflagging devotion to poetry in the region, Emerald Street Poets, my writing & critique group of fellow poets, and Saddle Road Press, for their vision in supporting unconventional, cross-genre work.

Finally, I'm grateful to my loving and talented family, including my wife Linda Kittle, daughter Kelsey, son Gabe, and the rest of the marvelous clan.

About the Author

Dane Cervine's previous poetry books include *Kung Fu of the Dark Father*, *How Therapists Dance*, *The Jeweled Net of Indra*, and *What a Father Dreams*.

Dane's poems have won awards from Adrienne Rich, Tony Hoagland, the *Atlanta Review*, *Caesura*, and been nominated for a Pushcart. His work appears in *The SUN*, the *Hudson Review*, *TriQuarterly*, *Poetry Flash*, *Catamaran*, *Miramar*, *Rattle*, *Sycamore Review*, and *Pedestal Magazine*, among others. Visit his website at: www.DaneCervine.typepad.com.

Dane practices psychotherapy in Santa Cruz, California, where he lives with his wife and family. His long-time meditation practice and his study with the Pacific Zen Institute infuse his work.

www.ingramcontent.com/pod-product-compliance
Lightning Source LLC
Chambersburg PA
CBHW030440010526
44118CB00011B/721